WELCOME TO
TEEN Breathe

Tomorrow, next week, next month: it's easy to put off for another day a task that, well, just doesn't appeal that much or seems so daunting that even thinking about it can make you feel ill. The trouble is, delaying jobs – AKA procrastinating – tends to make them even less attractive and a lot more stressful.

There are ways to make things easier (*Teen Breathe*'s favourite is breaking them down into smaller, more manageable chunks). But it's just as important to open up about any underlying or additional worries you might have, be they fears about revising for mock exams or confusion because a friend's blanked you.

A parent or guardian isn't always the go-to choice. They might appear to be on a totally different wavelength or be really busy with work and seem pretty stressed themselves. This doesn't, however, stop them wanting to be there for you.

So, choose a quiet moment and maybe tell them you'd appreciate their opinion. They'll love it (honestly) – and there's a good chance they'll be able to suggest some fresh ideas. Just try not to put it off for too long.

DON'T MISS YOUR NEXT ISSUE: ON SALE FROM 15 JANUARY 2019
FIND MORE INSPIRATION AT **TEENBREATHE.CO.UK**

LOOK AGAIN

Notions of beauty vary the world over, but the truth is that it's
what's on the inside that really matters – kindness, a generous spirit,
a smart brain – and that's what makes everyone uniquely beautiful

There's been a welcome change in recent years about how women are represented in the media. And thankfully, models with perfect makeup, petite waists and impossibly long legs are no longer the only kind you'll see. Today, a look at your favourite Instagram accounts or glossy magazines will increasingly show a fabulous diversity of all shapes and sizes. It's still possible to experience feelings of inadequacy, though, with thoughts popping up like: 'I don't look like that, and I'm never going to look like that.'

The wonderful truth, however, is you don't need to look like anyone other than yourself. Physical beauty is subjective – what one person finds beautiful might be very different to someone else.

In Japan, for example, a larger nose is considered handsome, while on the Indian Ocean island of Mauritius, the bigger you are, the better. To demonstrate this shifting perception of beauty, high-street store Superdrug asked female graphic designers from 18 different countries to manipulate a woman's image by making her 'more attractive to the people of their country'.

The results were staggering. In Italy, she was made taller and thinner; in Spain they made her larger and curvier; in China, she was made to look like a Barbie doll; in the Netherlands they gave her red hair; and in Egypt, her hair turned jet black. No single image looked the same, and no one perception of beauty could be called 'equal'.

Beauty through the ages

The same is true of history. Some of the earliest known representations of a woman's body are the Venus figurines – small statues from Europe dating back 25,000 years. These squat, large-breasted, large-stomached women are thought to represent the ideal of beauty at that time.

Fast forward several thousand years to the 17th and 18th centuries, and artists continued to portray women as curvy. Flemish painter Peter Paul Rubens became known for it, and the plump, voluptuous women he portrayed – known as Rubenesque – were held up as symbols of beauty.

Nowadays, some would consider these female bodies to be 'too large'. Yet what was considered beautiful in the 1970s – super-skinny women without much shape – would today be thought of as 'too thin'. The same goes for red hair, short hair, long hair, freckles, tattoos, being 'too muscular', 'too curvy', 'too short' and 'too tall'. There was a time when gapped teeth were thought of as 'ugly'; yet some of the world's best-known actors, such as Eddie Murphy, and models, like Lara Stone, rock the gap tooth with pride. Everyone's different, but being different doesn't somehow make you 'lesser'. It makes you individual.

It's an inside job

The trouble is, with selfies and social media, it's hard to escape the judgment of others. This makes everyone feel insecure, including those you'd expect to be confident. Even actress of the moment, Margot Robbie, who's been named as one of the most beautiful women in Hollywood, said in an interview with *Vanity Fair*: 'I am definitely not the best looking. I did not grow up feeling like I was particularly attractive. You should have seen me at 14, with braces and glasses, gangly and doing ballet!'

Similarly, Oscar-winning actress Lupita Nyong'o, who starred in the recent *Star Wars* movies, said in a speech about her childhood: 'I put on the TV and only saw white, pale skin. I was teased and taunted about my night-shaded skin and my one prayer to God was that I would wake up light-skinned.'

What's important to know is that beauty is about more than physical appearance. It's how you think and how you behave. Actions say far more than a nice haircut and tight-fitting dress. And we know beauty doesn't stay the same for long. So be confident in yourself, because confidence is the most beautiful quality of all.

WORDS: OLIVIA LEE. ILLUSTRATIONS: ANIESZKA BANKS

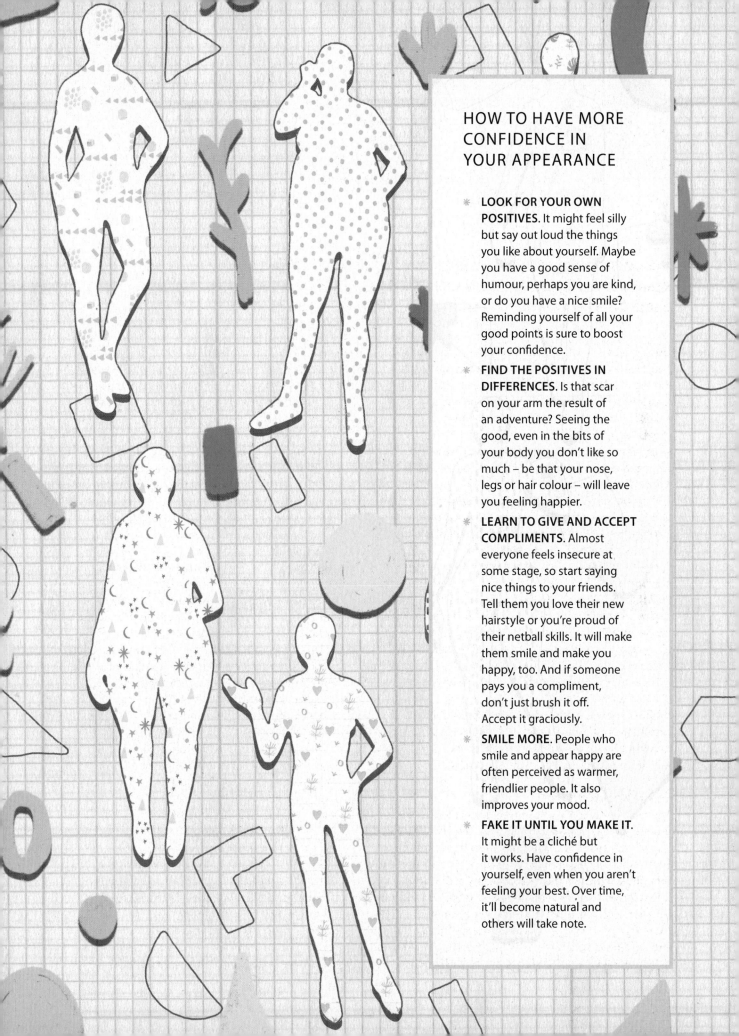

HOW TO HAVE MORE CONFIDENCE IN YOUR APPEARANCE

* **LOOK FOR YOUR OWN POSITIVES**. It might feel silly but say out loud the things you like about yourself. Maybe you have a good sense of humour, perhaps you are kind, or do you have a nice smile? Reminding yourself of all your good points is sure to boost your confidence.

* **FIND THE POSITIVES IN DIFFERENCES**. Is that scar on your arm the result of an adventure? Seeing the good, even in the bits of your body you don't like so much – be that your nose, legs or hair colour – will leave you feeling happier.

* **LEARN TO GIVE AND ACCEPT COMPLIMENTS**. Almost everyone feels insecure at some stage, so start saying nice things to your friends. Tell them you love their new hairstyle or you're proud of their netball skills. It will make them smile and make you happy, too. And if someone pays you a compliment, don't just brush it off. Accept it graciously.

* **SMILE MORE.** People who smile and appear happy are often perceived as warmer, friendlier people. It also improves your mood.

* **FAKE IT UNTIL YOU MAKE IT.** It might be a cliché but it works. Have confidence in yourself, even when you aren't feeling your best. Over time, it'll become natural and others will take note.

THE MAGIC OF HALT

Keeping on top of your emotions can be hard, but here's one way
to help make sure you're in control when it matters most

Life is a complicated business and there are moments when it can be really difficult to keep your emotions in check. Sometimes they may take over completely and you say or do something that you didn't mean.

It happens. You're not the first person to lose control and you won't be the last. But it's important to know that there are certain things you can do to make sure you're ready to deal with an important conversation or an exam, make a big life decision, or tackle something that really matters to you.

There is a checklist, called HALT, that can help you decide whether you're in the best state of mind to approach a particular situation and, if that situation can't be avoided, whether you need to do something to improve your chances of dealing with it in an appropriate way.

What is HALT?

HALT stands for Hungry, Angry, Lonely, Tired. These are all feelings that can hijack your emotions and affect the parts of the brain that control logical thinking, reasoning and problem-solving.

If you're feeling any of these things, it can be hard to think clearly and it's easier for your more instinctive emotions to take over. In order to recognise and tackle your HALT areas before they start running the show, you can ask yourself a key question: am I hungry, angry, lonely or tired?

If you are, then taking action can have a significant impact on how you manage the situation. The sections below explain what's going on in these areas and how to conquer any difficulties they present.

Hungry

Don't underestimate the power of hunger to mess with emotions. Without regular, balanced meals, the brain may start to become preoccupied by food and your blood sugar levels might dip, which can lead to mood swings and irritability.

Naomi Buff, a holistic nutritional wellness coach from Naomi's Kitchen, says: 'It is important to have three balanced meals a day, particularly eating a good-quality breakfast within two hours of waking up.'

She says that your choice of snacks during the day is also important as they can affect blood sugars and mood. Her suggestions include hummus with veggie sticks, homemade energy balls or rice cakes with almond butter.

Angry

If you feel angry, it can be helpful to reflect on what triggered it in the first place. Can you do something about this situation now? If yes, make a plan and take steps to put it into action – maybe you could apologise to the friend you might have upset or finish the homework that you started.

If you have to wait to put the plan into action, decide when you'll do it. If you can't do anything about the situation now, it's time to let it go and move on to something else.

Imagine blowing the problem away on a bubble or write it down on a piece of paper, rip it up and put it in the bin. Find something enjoyable and active to occupy your time and your thoughts, so you're not just going over it in your mind.

Lonely

Feeling lonely can seriously colour your thoughts. Being around other people generates mood-enhancing chemicals and also helps to prevent your view of life from becoming narrow and negative. If you notice your mood taking a turn for the worse and you think it may be because you're feeling lonely, make contact with someone you enjoy being around.

Tired

Whether you've been overdoing it or your sleep's been disrupted by next-door's dog barking all night, tiredness can affect mood. Think about your bedtime habits. Are you going to bed early enough or waking up worried about something?

Try keeping a notebook by the side of your bed and jot down anything important you need to do or things that are worrying you. This will get those thoughts out of your head and help you get some restful sleep, knowing that none of the important details will be forgotten.

HALT your patterns

These aren't the only things that can affect your mood, but the HALT checklist is a great place to start. Keeping a diary of your moods (and what you do to manage them) can help you become more familiar with your emotional patterns and could even prevent some problems from arising time and time again. You might make some surprising discoveries, too – for instance, could it be that every time you get annoyed with your sibling it also happens to be when you really need to have something to eat?

WORDS: DR SARAH MAYNARD. ILLUSTRATIONS: STEPHANIE GINGER

TEARS OF

Bursting into tears when something good happens might seem weird, but leaping (and weeping) for joy is a common and natural response that is expressive and can even be good for your health

WHY DO PEOPLE CRY WHEN THEY'RE HAPPY?

Despite plenty of scientific studies, nobody knows for certain why some cry tears of joy while others stay dry-eyed. It depends upon the individual and how they feel in any given situation.

Emotion, which is basically energy in motion, is a powerful response to life's everyday events and happenings. Some people are more sensitive than others and feel things more acutely. As a result, their emotional response can be heightened. Often, they cry easily, sometimes for the slightest thing, and especially at key moments in life. Perhaps you've seen this in people you know, or perhaps this applies to you directly.

It's thought that the brain registers intense emotion, whether happy or sad, as simply the same energy and responds the same way through tears. When the nerve receptors are activated, the brain's limbic system, which is connected to emotional responses, stimulates the gland that produces tears. So when an emotional threshold is reached, the tears simply flow.

This suggests that it's natural for everyone to express tears of sadness as well as joy. Not everyone finds it easy to cry, or even wants to express themselves, however, especially in public. Some might admit to 'filling up' or feel like they're 'close to tears'; others will choke them back; and more will bawl their eyes out. Whether you let tears of joy flow depends upon the way you feel and your emotions. Everyone is different and either response is fine.

RELEASING BUILT-UP EMOTIONS

Crying when happy can be a form of relief. For example, if you find yourself crying because you achieved the exam results you worked so hard for, the tears could be an expression and a release of the challenges and frustration you experienced while learning and revising. Similarly, if you cry because you've won an award or triumphed at a sporting event, those tears of joy are also likely to be sprinkled with the memory of the pain and hardship you went through to secure your success. It's why you often see professional athletes crying when they've won a medal or achieved their personal best.

Some psychologists believe that whatever the reason for crying, allowing the tears to flow helps to restore emotional harmony. It acts as a release valve, letting go of tension and stress you might not even be aware you were carrying.

Do you and your friends sometimes laugh so much that you cry?

It's thought that vigorous laughing puts pressure on the tear ducts resulting in reflex tears. Those tears rolling down your face are totally natural and even help to keep your eyes healthy.

WHAT TO DO WHEN YOU CRY TEARS OF JOY...

1 **If you feel like crying for joy, allow the tears to flow.** Sometimes, your eyes will fill up naturally before you've had a chance to think. Emotions are powerful and you might tremble as you well up with tears, so give yourself time to sit with your feelings. Notice how relaxed and free you are afterwards.

2 **There's no need to be embarrassed.** Tears, whether happy or sad, are a healthy response. If someone calls you names for crying or makes you feel uncomfortable, their response says more about them than you. It's quite possible they're bottling up or can't express their own feelings. Focus on what's right for you.

3 **Don't be surprised if your tears of joy make other people cry too.** It's quite natural. You'll all end up with tears rolling down your cheeks but this will open the way to smiles, laughter, stronger relationships and deep contentment.

WORDS: CAROL ANNE STRANGE. ILLUSTRATION: SARA THIELKER

LET GO OF YOUR EMOTIONS

Instead of bottling up your feelings, try writing them down in the space here. Let this be your release valve...

BLANKED

What should you do when a friend suddenly ignores you?

It's a common experience: last week, you and your friend were hanging out after school, making plans for the weekend and endlessly texting. Suddenly, your friend is barely acknowledging your existence – your messages go unanswered and they're avoiding you at school.

Why is this happening?
This behaviour is easier to understand, even if not easy to deal with, when there's a clear reason for it – if you've had an argument, for example. What's harder to handle is when your friend's sudden cold treatment has come from

nowhere. You scroll back through message threads and rummage in the corners of your mind for signs of recent trouble – only to draw a blank. What's going on?

It's important to realise that a friendship, like any relationship, has its ups and downs. Sometimes, a friend blanking you may just be one of those downs. As hurtful and bewildering as this feels, it may be a phase in the friendship's natural pattern. That said, your feelings matter, so it's important to identify what's going on and how you can either improve the situation or, if that's not possible, protect yourself against it.

How do I know if I'm being blanked?

Being blanked can take many forms. Are you being ignored? Is your friend consistently failing to answer your messages or return your calls? Are they walking straight past you without uttering a word or turning their back on you in a group situation and talking very obviously about things or events in which you're not involved? Being totally shunned in this way, both publicly and privately, can be upsetting and humiliating.

Trickier to interpret are actions involving delay – like when you message a friend and they take a lot longer than usual to reply, or when you suggest doing something together and they respond vaguely, rather than enthusiastically.

There's no sense in getting anxious if this happens once or twice – after all, everybody has times when their phone is dead or they have to check other commitments before they can give a definite answer.

Similarly, if you find yourself face to face and your friend acts unnaturally or appears to make excuses to end the encounter, don't fret – they may just have other things on their mind. If a pattern starts to emerge, however, it may be that your friend is taking a deliberate step back from your friendship. Either way, be sure to weigh up it all up carefully before jumping to conclusions.

What's going on with them?

As hurt or abandoned as you feel, take a moment to put yourself in the other person's shoes. Could they be going through a really busy or stressful time? Are they shutting down because something is causing them distress? Even if you haven't had a fight, have you said or done something that's made its way back to them? Try to think about your actions objectively: something that you consider harmless could have been interpreted differently by your friend.

What should I do?

Accusing your friend of blanking you could potentially make the situation worse. So, tempting as it may be to bombard them with messages and questions, it may be better to give them space. Instead of an approach that may come across as defensive or aggressive ('Why are you ignoring me?'), try something more along the lines of 'You don't seem yourself. Is everything okay?'. This gives your friend the opportunity to explain the situation to you. If they don't want to elaborate, it may be worth stepping back for a little while.

Safeguard yourself in all of this, too. It's considerate to give your friend time and space, but what about you? That time and space should not, at your end, be filled with fretting about what's going on.

Making time for yourself and what you enjoy is always important, but never more so than when you need to shield yourself from things you have no control over. Seek out other friends, engage in other hobbies, indulge in other treats. Get on with *your* life.

Rumination, obsession and stalking on social media are absolutely not your friends right now. Don't write off your friendship with that person, but don't let this situation consume you or define this moment in your life.

What can you learn from this?

There are life lessons to be learned from the bumps in the road of every relationship. For one thing, you learn you cannot control the behaviours of others.

These situations also give you an opportunity to examine your own behaviours, and you do have control over these. Do you sometimes push people away because you fear they're going to abandon you first? Are your friendships properly balanced or are you often in a position where you feel you hold less 'power'? This time of separation from the other person is a good space in which to look for patterns and think about ways to alter them.

When you talk again

In most cases, being blanked is temporary. If you still value your friendship and want it to continue, try to make the first few interactions you have afterwards face-to-face ones – texts are easily misinterpreted.

Be honest about how the episode has made you feel. If you know that you've done nothing wrong, try not to apologise just to get things back to normal, as you'll be helping to create a dynamic of imbalance in the future – and most likely setting yourself up for repeat episodes of blame.

If, however, you can see that you're at fault in some way, accept and acknowledge that responsibility and apologise for it sincerely. This is a time to reboot your friendship, to make it work for both of you, and to look to the future.

WORDS: SARAH RODRIGUES. ILLUSTRATION: CELESTE WALLAERT

HANG IN THERE

Failure is a hard thing to come to terms with. It can make you feel powerless and alone. And if it happens more than once, it's easy to think that you'll never be able to succeed and it might be better to give up altogether. Try to look at things differently. Success is within your grasp and overcoming obstacles is a talent that will help you develop as a person

Struggles are the essence of life

Can you imagine a life in which everything came easily? You wouldn't have to face life-changing decisions, stand up for what you believe in, or even work hard to reach your goals. Wouldn't that be great?

The obvious answer may be 'yes', but it's not quite that simple: without goals and dreams to fight for, life's journey would be pretty boring and even a bit meaningless. Challenges can be a positive part of life and provide focus.

Tackling obstacles head-on tests capabilities and builds character. Challenges give you a sense of purpose, motivating you to succeed. They may test patience and self-belief along the way, but they allow you to appreciate what you have.

The tests you face today will also prepare you for the future. Try to accept them for what they are and see if you can change your attitude towards what some people think of as failure – they can be real learning experiences.

'Fall seven times, stand up eight'

This powerful Japanese proverb says it all: life will knock you down more than once and it's up to you to get back up. It's really not about standing up the first time, but about persevering fall after fall. Keep getting up and moving on, no matter what life throws at you, and eventually you'll succeed.

It might be hard when you're in the middle of testing times, but try to be optimistic and don't be afraid of getting it wrong along the way.

Mistakes are an opportunity to learn and grow. If you fail, don't be defeated. Have another go and try to recognise where it went wrong last time. Try to find an alternative route to reach your goal – maybe, as the proverb says, you'll make it the eighth time and it will all be worthwhile.

Any cause for celebration

Highlight your progress – not your disappointments. Recognise you're on the right track and appreciate each step forward as a small victory that will get you even closer to your final goal.

If you look at a mistake as feedback, rather than a setback, you can learn more from it. You can then use this knowledge to challenge yourself to find another way. It might mean stepping out of your comfort zone for a while, but you'll end up being proud of the courage you've shown.

Most successful people have had to make sacrifices and overcome problems on their way to the top. Perseverance, passion, curiosity and imagination are all qualities that can help you push yourself beyond your own expectations.

There are lots of famous people who could easily have given up before they made their mark. You may have heard of James Dyson, who makes vacuum cleaners. It took him 15 years and 5,000 prototypes before he found one that he could sell. Now his company sells millions.

JK Rowling, who wrote the Harry Potter books, was rejected by 12 publishers before one finally agreed to print her story. Those books went on to sell 450 million copies.

If you surrender, you throw away your chance of success. If you keep trying and focus your efforts in the right direction, you can reach your full potential. You may falter, but make sure you also celebrate your successes, however small they seem.

Let YOUR Dream BE BIGGER than Your ~ FEARS ~

BELIEVE
IN YOUR DREAMS

Ambition can be a driving force for life. Believe in your dreams and have a good try at fulfilling them. As the famous saying goes: *'If at first you don't succeed, try, try again.'*

Perseverance is key
Once you've established a goal you truly want to achieve, keep going for it and be self-aware. Analyse each setback as it happens and identify any patterns. If the approach you're using isn't working, try a different one until you find a method or a strategy that works best for you.

Anything is possible… with planning and self-belief
Discovering a solution to the problems that are holding you back will make you see and believe that anything's possible. Devising a proper plan is essential, but also trust your instincts, especially if you're struggling to find answers.

Look at the bigger picture
If you hit a wall, don't give up. Think of a way around it, or under it, or over it. This may mean looking at the bigger picture and changing direction or adapting your goals. Rethinking your route is a brave decision and certainly not a failure. It's another milestone on your journey.

Happy accidents
What if you look at the situation with fresh eyes? Stop focusing exclusively on finding solutions. Mistakes can also offer you new opportunities out of the blue, just by luck. If you are open-minded and ready to explore new ideas, you may find unexpected success… and by pure mistake.

BRILLIANT MISTAKES
(top five unintentional inventions)

Tea bags: When a merchant sent out samples of tea in pretty silk bags, people started dropping them straight into the water
Penicillin: Mould found growing in a dirty Petri dish led scientists to the discovery of antibiotics
Post-it Notes: When an inventor tried to create a super-strong adhesive, he accidentally developed a reusable glue that made a great bookmark
Silly Putty: Attempts to design an alternative to rubber didn't go according to plan, but the result turned out to be a great toy
The microwave oven: A scientist working for a company making radar equipment noticed that microwaves had melted his candy bar, and used them to heat food

WORDS: ANNE GUILLOT. ILLUSTRATION: SHUTTERSTOCK.COM

MY SUCCESS BOARD

Use this page to make a note of your goals and the steps you'll need to take to get there. Highlight any successes as you go – no matter if they're small or large. If you hit any hurdles, you can come back and adapt your plans. Keep going and make your dreams a reality.

BEATING BETRAYAL

How to cope when those you trust break your confidence

Being betrayed is one of the most painful feelings in the world. It can shake you to your core, affect your ability to trust others and leave you feeling vulnerable or exposed.

Betrayal can come in many forms, but ultimately it's when someone you love and trust does something that hurts you deeply. You may feel betrayed if your parents split up or start seeing other people; a friend reveals your secrets; or someone talks about you behind your back. It can leave you angry and questioning your relationship with the person who's hurt you. It can also damage your faith in others as you end up wondering if they'll betray you next.

Why do people hurt those they love?

There isn't a definitive answer to why people betray others. People change, people make mistakes. Sometimes those you love aren't the people you think they are. Betrayal means the deliberate act of hurting someone, but sometimes you may feel betrayed even when the person who has upset you hasn't done it with that intention.

People who betray others are often overcome by a sense of ambition, greed or passion and when they can't control these things, they may do something that causes them to betray those they love. For example, a friend's desire to be part of the in-crowd could mean they reveal secrets or share information given to them in strictest confidence just so they can get into the gang.

When someone is determined to do or get something, nothing can stand in their way – even if it means betraying those closest to them. In relationships, powerful emotions can change people and make them behave differently.

WAYS TO OVERCOME THE PAIN OF BETRAYAL

1 Don't bottle up your feelings
If you don't discuss how the betrayal has made you feel, it might have negative effects in the future. For example, it could disrupt your sleep patterns, affect your mental health or prevent you trusting others. Feeling betrayed hurts, so allow yourself to cry, shout and think about the situation for a while. It's natural to be upset in these circumstances.

2 Write it down
Take the time you need to consider what emotions you're experiencing and write down how you feel. You may also want to write a letter to the person who's hurt you, explaining exactly how you feel – but don't send it. Wait a week or so and re-read it before deciding whether or not to pass it on as you may find your feelings have changed, too. Even if the letter is solely for your own eyes, you'll find that just writing the words down can make you feel better.

3 Avoid retaliating
It's normal to want to get revenge on the person who betrayed you, but don't react quickly. Actions and words that come from a place of anger and hurt could be ones you end up regretting. Take time to process what's gone on and think the situation through. Look after yourself first.

4 Talk to someone
Discussing the situation can help you clear your mind and start the healing process. If you're finding it hard to get over the hurt and feel it's affecting you and that you can't switch off from it, talk to a trusted adult – it might be a guardian, an auntie or uncle, or the school counsellor – who will be able to advise you and suggest where to get extra help if it's needed.

5 Forgive and forget?
This may seem hard but, depending on the particular circumstances and how much the person means to you, give it time – it will benefit your mental health if you're able to forgive the person involved. It doesn't mean you accept what they did is right or forget it – but it will allow you some control of the situation in your mind and help to enable you to move on. If you have hate and anger in your head for too long, it can end up hurting you more than you realise and drain your emotions.

6 Listen to the person
If the person who's hurt you wants to talk to you, it may help you if you listen to them. They might admit their mistakes and ask for forgiveness or have things to say that make you look at the situation differently. Take time to consider their words. If you still want them in your life, you'll have to forgive them at some point.

7 Trust others
Just because one person has betrayed you, it doesn't mean everyone will. Surround yourself with positive, honest friends to remind yourself that betrayal is rare. Don't allow one person to affect how you see others. Continue to be brave and trusting and you'll see that most people in the world are good-hearted, just like you.

WORDS: DONNA FINDLAY. ILLUSTRATIONS: CLAIRE VAN HEUKELOM

One of your friends makes a comment you don't agree with, a shop overcharges you, or a teacher misunderstands you, what would your response be? Perhaps you'd get annoyed but shy away from saying anything, or maybe you'd be at the other end of the spectrum altogether, ranting and raving at anyone who will pay you attention.

Being assertive means getting the balance right between being too quiet and passive, or too loud and aggressive. Assertive behaviour acknowledges your needs – as well as those of others – and communicates what they are without apologising, either for them or your emotions.

Your may feel your assertiveness skills aren't too strong at the moment, but the good news is they can be developed and refined, so you can stand your ground and show your thoughts and feelings matter too.

Notice your patterns

The first step in developing assertiveness is to start looking at patterns of behaviours and responses. Recognising that you go along with what other people want or think is often a key feature in passivity and means your needs are rarely met. Over time, this approach can build resentment, which can come out in angry bursts.

At the other end, do you notice yourself flying off the handle when you don't get your way or someone doesn't agree with everything you're saying? Everyone does it, but it seldom leaves you feeling good and, importantly, the other person probably stopped listening as soon as you got angry. Keep a note of your responses so you can see if there's a pattern emerging.

Watch your communication

In her book, *Presence*, Amy Cuddy suggests that powerful speech is a vital part of assertiveness and confidence. Rather than speaking quietly and rushing through what you're trying to say, this involves speaking up so others can hear you properly, making eye contact and taking your time. It's OK to pause and speak slowly.

Once you've spent some time practising this behaviour, look again at the words you're using. Are you forever apologising or keeping your true feelings to yourself? Tune in to how you're really feeling in your thoughts and emotions and watch out for physical signals from your body that can alert you to changing emotions (think butterflies in your stomach or your chest tightening).

Take a deep breath and share how you feel in response to someone else's behaviour. Then (here's the really brave bit) tell them how you'd like things to be different. Try using the 'I feel… when you… I would like…' framework in your conversation. For example, you might say: 'I feel sad when you don't invite me to your sleepovers. I'd really like us to hang out more again.'

What's your body language saying?

Even if your words sound more assertive, what's your body language telling the outside world? Other people will be able to work out your feelings from the way you hold your body and the manner in which you move.

Passive body language often involves sloping forward, and hanging your shoulders and head. You might walk slowly, have your arms crossed and make small movements.

Assertive body language displays confidence without aggression. According to Amy, this means standing up tall and straight; making big open gestures, such as having your arms out wide; standing rather than sitting when appropriate; and even placing your hands on your hips.

Our panel (below) has some poses you can practise before going into a new environment, having a difficult conversation or just when you need a boost.

Start believing you matter

While these tips can help to make huge strides towards assertiveness, the final ingredient is to start believing you truly matter and that what you think and say is important.

Developing your assertiveness is a way of taking some responsibility for your own needs and it signals to others how to treat you. The time for sinking into the shadows has passed, it's time to stand up and be counted and let the world know that you've arrived.

POWER POSES

WONDER WOMAN Hands on hips, feet hip-distance apart, chin slightly lifted.

OUTSTRETCHED ARMS Imagine you've just won a race, put your arms up in a wide 'V' in the air as if celebrating.

SUPERMAN Feet hip-distance apart, one hand on hip, other arm straight up in the air with fist clenched.

Hold your pose for at least 30 seconds. Give them a try when no one's watching – it might feel silly, but it can help you to feel more powerful.

WORDS: DR SARAH MAYNARD. ILLUSTRATION: ELLICE WEAVER

'I'LL DO IT LATER'

There can't be many students who haven't put homework off for another day, guitar practice for another week, or tidying their room for (at least) another month. It's rarely a disaster – there are occasions when there's no option but to delay a task and sometimes it works just as well (if not better) to do it later.

But there's an old saying you might have heard: 'Don't put off until tomorrow what you can do today' and (unfortunately) it does have quite a lot going for it. Why? Because endlessly putting off a task, or 'procrastinating', can increase stress levels and have an effect on your achievements.

Why tomorrow?

Be honest, not all tasks are created equal. Let's say you're given two instructions: 'Tidy your room' and 'Here's some money – order pizzas for you and your friends.' We know which one we'd put to the side. But people procrastinate for many reasons. It could be:

>> there's something about a task that is unappealing
>> it compares unfavourably to another activity you could be doing
>> your feelings around it are negative

So, you might put off studying for a science test because:

>> you don't like the subject
>> you'd rather be with your friends at the park
>> your nerves about the test are so great that you don't even want to think about it

When is it a problem?

Putting something off until later isn't always an issue (some people even work better when they have a deadline looming). Postponing a task isn't always procrastination, either – like when the dog needs a walk but it's raining heavily so you wait until the weather clears up.

By the same token, short-term procrastination of the 'I just don't feel like it' type may not be a problem – who doesn't hit the snooze button a few times before getting out of bed? When the delay becomes more long term, however, it can have a knock-on effect. This could be when you press snooze too many times, make yourself late and then end up starting your day stressed and frazzled.

Think ahead

Often the problem with procrastination is that it can make tasks seem overwhelming, even the pleasant ones.

Take Christmas presents, for example. Say you have 10 to buy for your friends and you have to hand them all out on the last day of term. You could spend a couple of days thinking about what each friend might like and then buy two each weekend in the five weeks leading up to the festive break. That's two per weekend over five weeks – not so bad.

Delay the task for too long and those numbers creep up. Two becomes four, four turns into six and then before you know it you have only one weekend to find 10 gifts that you know your mates will like and you're really happy with.

Schoolwork's the same. Suppose you have two weeks to complete an assignment. It's a difficult one and you're not feeling confident about it, so you leave it until later. Before you know it, you have only a week left to do it, which instantly makes it seem even more overwhelming and difficult. Perhaps at this point you put it off further, and end up rushing to get it done the day before the due date. This can result in more stress and possibly a lower mark than the one you could have achieved.

What's the solution?

Realising when procrastination is a problem is the first step to tackling the issue. Take the example of the assignment, for instance. If the stress and (possibly) a lower mark than the one you know you could have achieved dent your confidence, you might repeat the same pattern next time you have a similar test – and, without meaning to, put yourself in an unhelpful cycle or pattern of behaviour.

If, on the other hand, you look at the situation and see that starting the assignment earlier might have meant less stress and a higher mark, then you can decide to change things. The important thing is not to give yourself a hard time. Accept that it happened and try to think of ways to tackle less appealing tasks in the future. Here are a few methods we use at the *Teen Breathe* office:

Manage your time: Create a timetable around activities, whether they're things you *want* to do (write a *Teen Breathe* feature) or things you *need* to do (read the final page proofs). It will help to organise yourself in a way that means you fit everything in and manage your time effectively.

Break tasks into blocks: Dividing a large task (checking all of *Teen Breathe*'s pages before they go to print) into several smaller ones (reading eight or nine pages a day over a week) makes everything seem more manageable. In a similar way, you could tidy your room area by area over a week or write a paragraph or so of your assignment each day. Start small and things will gain their own momentum.

Rewards: Every time you complete a section of the task, give yourself a break to do something else (sit in the *Teen Breathe* garden with a coffee) but keep an eye on timings.

If you still leave something until the last minute: Remember – 'better late than never'. See it as a challenge and do your best (read all of *Teen Breathe*'s pages in one day and hope there aren't too many spelling mistakes).

WORDS: SARAH RODRIGUES. ILLUSTRATION: SAMANTHA NICKERSON

CENTRE POINT

Creating your own mandala is a great way to relax

What is a mandala?

A mandala – translated as 'circle' in the ancient Asian language of Sanskrit – is a spiritual symbol dating back to early Hindu and Buddhist cultures. Traditionally used to symbolise the universe, mandalas were illustrations, generally in the form of a circle or geometric shape, with decorative images designed around a central point.

As well as being attractive, mandalas were a tool for focusing the mind – known as meditating – with the central point helping to aid concentration.

LET'S GET CREATIVE

Why not have a go at creating a mandala of your own? As well as the satisfaction of seeing the result of something you've created with your own hands, the process of being creative can have a positive effect on mental and emotional health. In the same way that mandalas can be used as a focal point for meditation, by engaging in a creative pastime the mind is given a focal point, which can help with relaxation. It doesn't matter if you think you're artistic or good at painting because this is more about the creative process than the finished product.

Materials

There are many things that can be used as a base for your mandala: a stone found on a walk, an old piece of fabric or even a fallen leaf in the park. Wherever possible, look for the most environmentally friendly option and consider how you might create a mandala from something that might otherwise be thrown away or left unloved.

Look for water-based paints and try to avoid anything oil-based, which might contain chemicals. You could ask a relative for leftover tins of paint or tester pots from household projects. There are also many good-quality, yet inexpensive paints and brushes – and good advice – available from local arts and crafts shops.

Be inventive with your materials. Try applying paint in new ways, for example, using the non-bristled end of your paintbrush to achieve a sharp, precise dot. Or get your hands dirty and smudge the paint with your fingers.

Give it time

There's no rush. Take time to connect with the process. Notice how the material feels in your hand. Observe the brush as you dip it in to the paint and glide its bristles along the surface of your base. Enjoy seeing the result of mixing different colours together. Your mandala doesn't have to be finished in one sitting – build it up gradually.

More often than not, the end result is quite different from the creative work envisioned, but don't let this put you off. Some of the most famous masterpieces were the result of artistic 'mistakes', so you'll be in great company.

The gift of giving

Don't underestimate the power that gifting something you've created can have. A beautiful, personalised mandala could be just the thing to brighten the day of a friend, family member or teacher. A handmade gift can mean so much more than something purchased from a shop (it's also a great way to save your pocket money for other treats). Or, if you have painted a stone you found locally, then maybe return it to the place where you found it for a lucky passer-by to admire during their morning stroll.

Allow your creative juices to flow, let your imagination run wild and enjoy being the centre of your own attention.

A simple structure of circles and lines can be your base

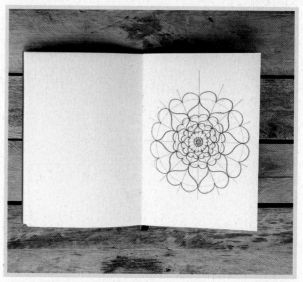

You could theme your mandala – love hearts, perhaps?

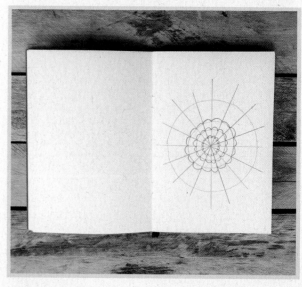

There's no rush – build up your mandala over time

WORDS: SIMONE SCOTT. ILLUSTRATIONS: LAURA BACKEBERG. PHOTOS: JOSH ALLISTON

BE LIGHT AND BRIGHT
like a butterfly

Butterflies are a beautiful, colourful reminder of the world's magic and miracles – research has shown they can even remember things learned in their caterpillar stage. Like the butterfly, people are constantly growing, developing and transforming into a greater version of themselves.

The butterfly pose in yoga – its Sanskrit name is *Baddha Konasana* – provides a lovely space to connect with your beautiful self. It strengthens and opens the hip area and stimulates energy flow to the lower abdominal area, easing cramps and discomfort and soothing the lower back.

HERE'S HOW TO GET INTO THE POSE:

1. Sit on the floor, legs outstretched. Hold the spine upright, tall and straight. Take a few gentle breaths to settle your mind and body.

2. On an out-breath, bend the knees and draw the feet towards the groin, bringing together the soles so they face each other. Gently wrap the hands around the feet, ankles or shin. Allow the inner thighs to relax and let the knees open downwards, towards the floor, as far as is comfortable.

3. Sitting up tall, broaden and lift the chest. Take a few deep breaths in this position and allow yourself to observe fully how you feel.

4. On an out-breath, fold the upper torso forward from the hips. If you can, rest the head on the soles of the feet. If not, fold forward as far as is comfortable. Take a few breaths, then lift the body back to sitting tall. Breathe and observe if this has helped to release tension on the lower back and made you feel more calm and relaxed.

One variation, which can be practised while sitting up tall at stage 3, is to move the knees gently up and down – a little like a butterfly flapping its wings.

We hope you enjoy practising the butterfly pose and find that it supports your transformation and liberation to being light, bright and free like a butterfly.

WORDS: DAWATTIE BASDEO – VISIT MAGNIFICENTMEMAGNIFICENTYOU.COM. ILLUSTRATION: SARA THIELKER

SHY *and* ASPIRING

If you find yourself tongue-tied and red-faced in social situations, you're not alone. Many people are bashful. Being shy is one of the many positive parts that make you who you are and there's no reason it should stop you achieving your dreams

The first couple of terms of the new school year are pretty much behind you now, and you may be confidently buzzing with the excitement of having more friends and a calendar bursting with invites.

If, however, you're bashful, those first weeks of the new year may have been painful. You may have felt tearful or panic-stricken at the thought of walking into a classroom full of unfamiliar faces, blushed or avoided eye contact whenever someone tried to speak to you, and spent your breaks sitting alone, beating yourself up about not being able to approach people to introduce yourself. You may have been thinking there was something wrong with you.

If that scenario sounds familiar, the first thing to know is there's nothing the matter with you. Shyness – broadly defined as feeling anxious around other people, and most intensely so in social situations such as your first day at school – is natural and many people, including those who seem most self-assured, experience from time to time.

WHERE DOES IT COME FROM?

Professor Joe Moran, author of *Shrinking Violets: The Secret Life of Shyness*, is an expert on the subject. Deeply shy himself, he says shyness is 'intrinsic' to being a human being.

'Humans are the only self-conscious species – that is, we alone are aware of ourselves and of how we relate and appear to others. To put it simply, what we call "shyness" arises from our desire to be liked.'

Though some people are shyer than others – it's believed to be hereditary – shyness can strike anyone at any time. It also ebbs and flows depending on context and situation, so you might be super chatty and open in one class, yet clam up in another if there are students, or a teacher, who make you feel less comfortable.

Even Kim Kardashian-West – seemingly one of the most attention-seeking celebrities on the planet – admitted she felt shy at times. 'The real Kim is not outspoken and loud like everyone assumes,' she said, 'but actually shy and reserved. I'm the girl who's too nervous to dance in a nightclub.'

WILL IT AFFECT YOUR GOALS?

In short, no. Kim's quote reveals it's in no way a barrier to following your dreams and fulfilling your ambitions. Singers Lady Gaga and Zayn Malik, actors Keira Knightley and Robert Pattinson, and writers JK Rowling and Hayley Scott are among the many successful people who are also bashful. It's something worth bearing in mind the next time you find yourself fretting about walking into a coffee shop on your own or going to a party.

CAN SHYNESS BE GOOD?

In short, yes. Shyness is one of the (many) characteristics that make you, you, so you should necessarily seek to change it.

Professor Moran sees it as a personality trait, just like being conscientious or open, and one that has many positives. For example, shy people are often good listeners, more contemplative and empathetic. Their actions and speech are considered, so what they say and do is unlikely to change on a whim, which makes them dependable and constant.

WAYS TO COPE

While accepting that being shy is part of your nature, finding ways to control it may be helpful. Professor Moran says: 'I fully accept my shyness but felt that having some coping mechanisms would enable me to function more comfortably in social situations.'

1 Plan ahead

'Shy behaviour can sometimes be misinterpreted as aloofness, which can make forming friendships more difficult initially, so I've moderated how I meet and greet people,' adds Professor Moran. 'I smile, I plan conversations and I carry a notebook with things to say in case I run out of small talk, which helps me feel more secure.'

2 Ease yourself into uncomfortable situations

Since shyness is really a fear – of drawing attention to or making a fool of yourself, or of being rejected – it might help to confront it. If you can prove to yourself that your fears are unfounded, they'll lose their power over you.

The only way to do this, of course, is to do the things that scare you. Start gently, perhaps by vowing to yourself that the next time you're in a group of strangers, you'll say hello first to just one person. If that's too much, ease yourself in, by walking into a room and smiling at people.

3 Practise

The trick is to keep practising being more outgoing – in other words, to fake it until you make it. If you speak to one person at one event, try speaking to two people the next time, then three, and so on. In time, you'll become outwardly less shy despite the anxiety you may still feel within.

Where to get help

If your social anxiety is preventing you from making friends and enjoying your life, please speak to a trusted adult. They may suggest you'll grow out of it, and they're right – people do tend to become less shy as they mature – but help is available now.

MoodJuice publishes an excellent self-help guide on shyness and social anxiety (moodjuice.scot.nhs.uk/ shynesssocialphobia.asp); Childline (childline.org.uk, 0800 1111) is packed with great advice on many subjects, including how to become more socially adept; and kidshealth.org has articles that will help you understand shyness better. If your social anxiety is extreme, it might be an idea to visit your GP.

Some general guidance:

* Try to talk about important things when you're feeling calm and have time – not as you're rushing off somewhere
* It can feel more comfortable to talk when you're side by side, such as when you're out and about in the car or walking
* Remember your parent/guardian is human too – there will be times when they feel tired, stressed or worried, so these are times to maybe avoid a 'big' talk
* Blaming doesn't help anyone – try to take responsibility for what's happened and how you're feeling. Instead of starting statements with 'You…', try leading with 'I…' statements, such as 'I feel…'

IT'S GOOD TO TALK

It may not always be easy chatting to a parent or guardian – but it can be worth it. Here, *Teen Breathe* explores how to get the best out of the conversation

Sometimes it can feel like you're on the exact same wavelength as a parent or guardian and other times it can feel like they don't understand the first thing about you. Even though there's plenty of times you need them and their help or advice, sometimes when you try to speak to them it just comes out as anger and frustration. The good news is that there are plenty of things you can do about this to help one of those chats run more smoothly.

When you want something
Starting a conversation with 'I really want…' or 'Everyone else has…' is unlikely to get a parent onside. Let them know this isn't an on-the-spot decision about something you need: this is an issue you've been thinking of for some time. Give thought-through, logical reasons why you need this thing – for example, you'd like to feel good about yourself by wearing something new; you'd like some games that would help you relax when you're not studying; or you'd really like to go to the festival because you feel it

would help increase your independence. Importantly, explain how you could contribute to or repay any cash. If you've worked out that from your Saturday job you can give £25 or you're going to spend the next two months saving up towards it, that shows you've given it thought. It'll be harder for them to argue against a sensible, logical plan.

When you need help with your emotions
Maybe you haven't received the exam results you'd hoped for or you've fallen out with a friend. It might not always feel like it, but parents and guardians want nothing more than to be included and help when big stuff happens. At times like this it may be hard to plan a calm conversation – perhaps tears and emotions might take over, but this is okay. Just tell them what happened and what's upset you. Letting them hug you might help. Giving them clues on how they can support you (or not) can be useful, too: 'I'm not sure what I want to do about this just yet, but it's been

WORDS: DR SARAH MAYNARD. ILLUSTRATION: STEPHANIE HOFMANN

useful chatting' or 'It would be really nice if we could just watch a film together tonight and forget about all of this for a while'.

When you feel like you're not being told something
Sometimes you just know information is being kept from you – and you're sure it's important. The chances are they feel it's either too big or inappropriate to tell you, or they don't know how to deal with it themselves.

A 'grown-up' approach is key here but it's got to be genuine. Let them know that you've noticed they're distracted or untalkative and ask if they're okay. They might be looking for the right time to tell you something. And if you can't do anything else, maybe leave a little note or gift for them – to let them know you're thinking of them.

When you're in trouble
Whether you've broken a valuable ornament or have a detention at school, you know you've got to come clean. Sit with a parent or guardian and let them know there's something you need to tell them. Open with the fact that you may be disappointed in yourself, but don't sugar-coat what's happened – give it to them straight. Give an indication that you know how they might be feeling hearing this: 'I know this will be a shock or disappointment'. Then tell them your plan for sorting out the situation – how you can fix or replace an item, for example, or how you've spoken to your teacher about completing extra school work.

And if all else fails…
If you've tried all the tips above and you're still not getting anywhere, don't think that you've failed. It might be that a parent or guardian has just too much going on and can't make themselves available to you right now.

Try again another time when you think that they might be in a better mood to listen. If this doesn't get you any further, you still don't have to give up. You could consider finding another adult you trust enough, perhaps an auntie or uncle, to talk to in the meantime.

A MEANINGFUL MESSAGE

With mobiles, email and social media quite literally at your fingertips, friends and family are rarely more than a touchscreen away. But did you know that there are advantages to traditional ways of keeping in touch, too? Experts say a simple card containing a heartfelt message could do wonders for a friend's wellbeing – and give your own a boost as well

What are the benefits?

In 2013, MindLab – an independent scientific research company – carried out a study into the effects of receiving handwritten greetings cards.

During a series of experiments, it showed the happiness response caused by greetings cards was twice as strong as that prompted when receiving a message via social media, and a whopping three times stronger than the reaction created by an email. Psychologists believe that this is partly because it takes effort and planning to send a card so, whether it's posted, put through a letterbox or popped on someone's desk, it shows the recipient that you appreciate and care for them.

The gift that keeps on giving

As a physical reminder of someone's good wishes, cards can help to reduce feelings of loneliness and isolation and, as they're designed to be displayed, they can continue to bring happiness for days, weeks or even years after they were originally sent.

Believe in your ability

A recent study by psychologists Kumar and Epley showed that, in the case of thank you cards, people tend to underestimate the positive effects their note will have on the recipient. Some even talk themselves out of sending one altogether because they believe they're 'not good enough' at writing and fear the note may cause embarrassment or awkwardness.

In fact, this couldn't be further from the truth. Evidence shows that even the simplest of thank you cards means a lot, often deeply touching the recipient and improving relationships. So, grab a pen and say what you mean.

TO MY FABULOUS FRIEND

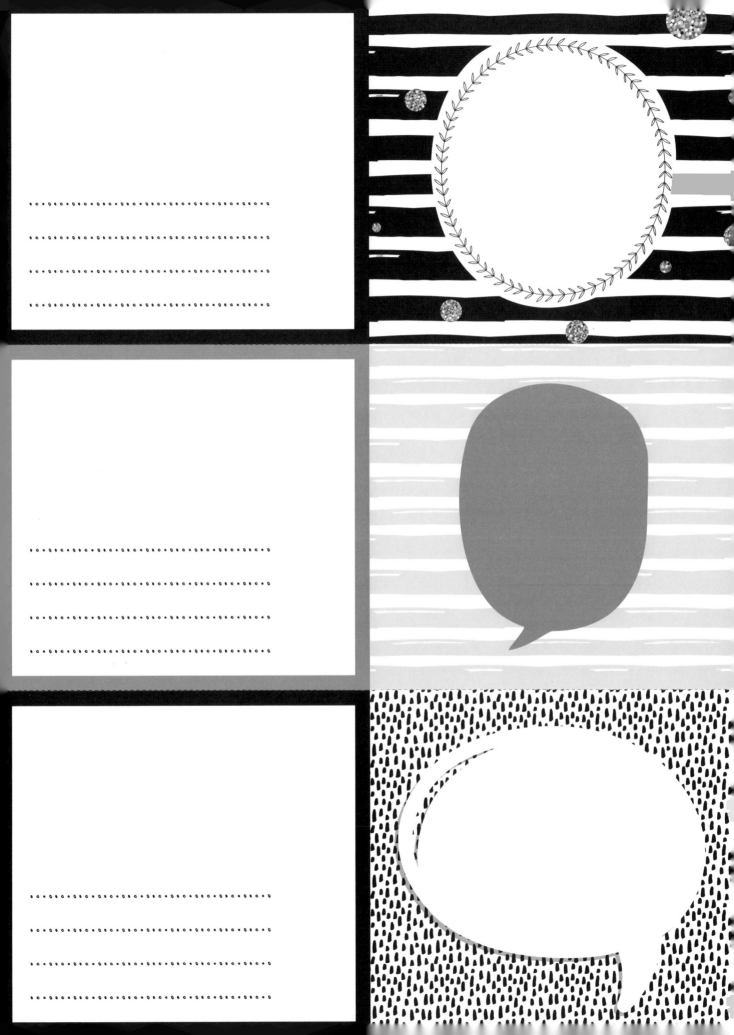

Joined-up thinking

There's no getting away from it: handwriting does take more effort than typing, but the good news is that joined-up writing has been shown to be far better for the writer than tapping away at a keyboard. It engages more of the brain and improves focus and memory. What's more, your handwriting is totally individual, making the note extra personal. When a card is handwritten, it shows the sender has sat down for a few minutes, without distraction, to truly concentrate on their message – a gift in itself when life's so busy.

It's personal

If handwriting alone is not enough of a personal touch, you could also make your card from scratch. It's a really popular craft and stationers and art shops have tons of card-making equipment. Again, don't allow self-doubt to hold you back – this truly is a case of it being the thought that counts. From a quick doodle to an intricate collage – your card can be as simple or as complicated as you like. The most important thing? You enjoy the process of making it.

The 'green' bit

Happily, there are a growing number of environmentally friendly greetings card makers – you can even find cards with wildflower seeds embedded in them. As a general, eco-conscious rule, try to buy cards that contain recycled or sustainably sourced paper (look for the FSC or PEFC logo) and, if you can find cards that are printed using low- or no-alcohol inks or vegetable inks, then so much the better.

With all of these plus points, perhaps it's not quite time to give up on old-fashioned communication just yet. Keep a small supply of cards handy and you'll always be prepared to pen a spontaneous note, sending someone a smile and spreading significantly more happiness than you might think. You can't ask more from your mail than that.

IN NEED OF INSPIRATION?

Here are a few great reasons to send a card:

Thank you – Is there an auntie or uncle who helped you with a project or supported you through your exams? Perhaps a neighbour or teacher has gone above and beyond to make your life easier. A thank you card could be the perfect way to show your appreciation.

Thinking of you – It's not always possible to be with your friends when they're going through a tough time, so a note can let them know you're thinking about them and sending them lots of love.

Fab friend – Maybe you have a friend who just needs to know how fabulous they are. Tell them how much they brighten your day, and you're sure to brighten theirs, too.

Ready to get writing? Use our free cards to let friends and family know you care

STIR IT UP!

OK, it probably won't happen too often, but if you find yourself at a loose end of a weekend, you could do far worse than to head to the kitchen to indulge in a spot of baking. It's a great way of giving tired eyes a break from reading, it can help to take your mind off any ongoing worries and is a welcome distraction from homework – at least, for a period of time. Pop some music on, too, and, voila, you have an unbeatable combination.

Don't worry if your cakes and biscuits aren't perfect either. Baking's all about trial and error. The important thing is to enjoy the process – you could even enlist some help from a sibling or your mum or dad if you want to make it a sociable time – and remember to share the goodies.

The rest of the family will likely be keen to help you polish them off, but if there are any left over, you could always take them into school for friends. A homemade cake will make Monday seem a whole lot better.

Here at *Teen Breathe,* we've decided that our next weekend baking session is going to involve one of these tasty recipes from Cath Kidston's *Mug Cakes, Cupcakes & More.*

We'll probably opt to make the Billionaire's Shortcake first as we can cover it in edible stars, wrap a few of the squares in pretty paper, tie them up with ribbon and give them to friends and family as delicious homemade gifts (not that we're after brownie points or anything).

STRAWBERRY CHEESECAKE CUPCAKES

MAKES 12

For the cakes
* 125g unsalted butter, softened
* 125g golden caster sugar
* 2 large eggs
* 125g self-raising flour
* 1 tsp baking powder
* ½ orange, finely grated zest
* 2 tbsp milk
* 100g strawberries, hulled and chopped into small pieces

For the icing and decoration
* 50g unsalted butter, softened
* 150g cream cheese, at room temperature
* 4 tbsp icing sugar
* 1 vanilla pod, seeds scraped out
* ½ ginger biscuit, crushed into crumbs
* 12 strawberries, halved or sliced

Preheat the oven to 180°C/350°F/gas 4. Line a 12-hole muffin tin with paper cupcake cases.

To make the cakes
1 Place the butter and sugar in a bowl and beat with an electric whisk until pale and fluffy.
2 Add the eggs, one at a time, beating well between each addition.
3 Sift over the flour and baking powder. Fold in with a metal spoon.
4 Add the orange zest, milk and strawberries and fold together.
5 Divide the mixture evenly between the paper cases and smooth the tops with the back of a spoon.
6 Bake for 18 minutes, or until well risen and slightly springy to the touch.
7 Remove the cakes from the tin and transfer to a wire rack to cool.

To make the icing
1 Beat together the butter, cream cheese, icing sugar and vanilla seeds until smooth.
2 When the cupcakes are cool, use a palette knife to spread the icing onto each cake.
3 Scatter with the biscuit crumbs, arrange a strawberry on top of each and serve immediately.

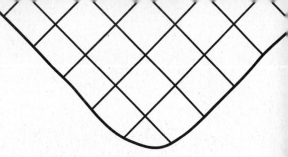

Preheat the oven to 180°C/350°F/gas 4. Line a 12-hole muffin tin with paper cupcake cases.

To make the cakes

1 Beat the butter and sugar with an electric whisk until pale and fluffy.
2 Add the eggs, one at a time, beating between each addition.
3 Sift over the flour and baking powder. Fold in using a metal spoon.
4 Add the vanilla extract and enough milk for the mixture to be of a dropping consistency.
5 Spoon half into a separate bowl and add the raspberries. Mash so the mixture is streaked pink, then set aside.
6 Stir the white chocolate into the non-raspberry mixture.
7 Place alternate dollops of the white chocolate and raspberry mixtures into the cupcake cases until the mixtures are evenly distributed.
8 Smooth the tops and bake for 18 minutes, or until well risen and springy to the touch.
9 Remove from the tin and transfer to a wire rack to cool.

For the white chocolate icing

1 Melt the chocolate, broken into squares, in 30-second bursts in the microwave, stirring between each burst, then set aside.
2 Beat the butter and icing sugar with an electric whisk until pale and fluffy, then beat in the melted chocolate until smooth.

For the dark chocolate icing

1 Melt the chocolate, broken into squares, in 30-second bursts in the microwave, stirring between each burst, then set aside.
2 Beat the butter, icing sugar and cocoa powder in a large bowl with an electric whisk until pale and fluffy. Then fold in the melted chocolate, milk and vanilla extract.

Spoon the white chocolate icing down one side of a piping bag fitted with a star nozzle and spoon the dark chocolate icing down the other side. Once the cupcakes are cool, pipe the icing onto the top of each cake, creating a marbled effect, and decorate with hearts and glitter. Top each one with a raspberry.

CHOCOLATE BERRY MARBLE CUPCAKES

MAKES 12

For the cakes
* 125g unsalted butter, softened
* 125g golden caster sugar
* 2 large eggs
* 125g self-raising flour
* 1 tsp baking powder
* 1 tsp vanilla extract
* 1-2 tbsp milk
* 100g raspberries
* 30g white chocolate, chopped

For the white chocolate icing
* 100g white chocolate
* 140g unsalted butter, softened
* 140g icing sugar

For the dark chocolate icing
* 100g good-quality dark chocolate (70 per cent cocoa solids)
* 150g unsalted butter, softened
* 200g icing sugar
* 3 tbsp cocoa powder
* 2-3 tbsp milk
* 2 tsp vanilla extract

To decorate
* Chocolate hearts
* Edible glitter
* 12 fresh raspberries

SALTED CARAMEL BILLIONAIRE'S SHORTCAKE

MAKES 16-20 SQUARES

For the bottom layer
* 300g digestive biscuits
* 125g salted butter, melted

For the caramel layer
* 100g salted butter, plus extra for greasing
* 1 x 397g can condensed milk
* 75g light muscovado sugar
* 75g golden syrup
* 1 vanilla pod, seeds scraped
* Pinch of sea salt

For the top layer
* 150g good-quality dark chocolate (70 per cent cocoa solids), broken into squares
* 50g white chocolate, broken into squares
* Edible gold or silver stars

Edited extract from *Cath Kidston: Mug Cakes, Cupcakes & More* by Cath Kidston. Published by Quadrille, £15

Lightly grease a 20cm square baking tray and line it with baking paper.

To make the bottom layer
1 Place the digestives in a blender and blitz until they form crumbs. Pour in the melted butter and blitz until combined.
2 Tip the mixture into the prepared tin and press down to make an even layer. Place in the fridge while you prepare the caramel.

To make the caramel layer
1 Pour all the caramel ingredients into a saucepan, place over a low heat and stir constantly until melted. Keep a close eye on the mixture, keeping the heat low, and stir continuously as it can catch on the bottom of the pan.
2 Bring to a simmer and bubble for 10 minutes, or until the mixture starts to thicken and deepens to a darker caramel colour.
3 Discard the vanilla pod.
4 Pour the caramel over the biscuit base and leave to chill for at least two hours, until set.

To make the top layer
1 Place the dark chocolate in a microwaveable bowl and melt in 30-second bursts in the microwave, stirring between each burst.
2 Repeat with the white chocolate in a separate bowl.
3 Pour the dark chocolate over the whole of the cake.
4 Place dollops of the white chocolate on top of the dark chocolate.
5 Using a toothpick, swirl the top to create a marbled effect.
6 Sprinkle with gold or silver stars, cover and chill in the fridge for one hour, or until totally set.
7 Cut into squares to serve.

HANDLE WITH CARE

Life as a young carer can be rewarding, fulfilling and build self-esteem. But it can also be difficult and isolating. Remember to get the support you need to look after yourself, too

Agatha Christie, the writer best known for her detective novels, once said that 'one of the luckiest things that can happen to a person is to have a happy childhood'.

Growing up in a supportive and loving home, with at least one parent or guardian who looks after you, ensures you have a safe and clean place to live, a healthy diet and a shoulder to cry on, and that you can devote quality time to schoolwork, friends and yourself. Ultimately, it gives you the space to mature at your own pace, gradually taking on more responsibilities as and when you are emotionally ready. For many young people, however, life is different.

Sometimes unforeseen circumstances, such as serious mental or physical illness, can leave those who would otherwise be taking care of you unable to do so. This can reverse your role in the family, and put you in the position of carer. Suddenly you find yourself with grown-up responsibilities that might include washing, shopping, cleaning and looking after the person who's unwell and, sometimes, younger siblings.

Life as a young carer – defined legally as a person under 18 who looks after 'any family member who is physically or mentally ill, frail, elderly, disabled or misuses alcohol or substances' – can be rewarding. Young carers say looking after those they love gives them a sense of pride, self-worth and purpose and that they are more independent than their schoolfriends. But it can also be challenging and sometimes socially isolating.

School encounters

If you are in this position, there may be times when you feel lonely or think life is unfair. You may wish you had more time to yourself or have problems at school, like being mocked and left out of activities. In a 2013 survey for the Carers Trust, 25 per cent of young carers reported being bullied.

'Many of the children we deal with have had unpleasant experiences at school with their classmates poking fun at them for having a parent with physical or learning disabilities,

or mental health problems,' says Helen Leadbitter, National Young Carers Lead at The Children's Society.

'They can also be bullied because their life is different – they may not have the means or the time to socialise with peers or to dress nicely and they may be withdrawn – all of which make being part of the gang difficult.'

Rebecca McCann, who runs clickfortherapy.com, a counselling practice with a dedicated child and adolescent team, agrees. 'Young carers often have very different experiences to other children. While their friends are enjoying their childhoods, being cared for by their parent or parents, they have to deal with situations that are physically and emotionally draining.

'They may have to take the person they're caring for to hospital appointments, deal with social services, pay household bills and try to keep up their physical appearance, all while doing schoolwork and coping with the angst of growing up.'

It's common for young carers to feel marginalised and trapped by their situation. Some may be terrified of telling

a teacher, GP or someone in authority about what's going on at home, partly because they don't want to be disloyal to their family, and partly because they worry that they and their siblings might be taken into care.

You're not alone

If you're a young carer reading this, then know that you are definitely not alone and help – both emotional and financial – is available. Your welfare matters and you have the right to be looked after, too.

'The Office of National Statistics gave the official number of young carers in England and Wales in 2013 as 244,000,' says Helen. 'But we know that many more are hidden from view, so the real figure is likely to be significantly higher. There have been reports that there may be as many as 700,000 young carers in the UK.'

There's a good chance there will be other people in your school, perhaps even in your class, who are living this reality. If you're a carer, seeking out other young carers for mutual support would be a good first step, since being able to talk honestly to someone who understands your situation may help ease any anxieties you have.

Beyond that, please try to let your teacher know what's going on. Your school might be part of the Young Carers in Schools initiative, run by the Carers Trust and The Children's Society, which aims to provide support and help for people in your position. You are devoting a lot of time to other people that you love, but it is essential that you take care of yourself, too. There is support available so please do not try to shoulder this alone.

Where to go for help:

carers.org/about-us/about-young-carers
youngminds.org.uk
childrenssociety.org.uk/youngcarer/help-for-young-people

A PERSONAL STORY

Melissa Moody, who helped to look after several members of her family while she was still at school, recalls how the experience was challenging but helped her become a more independent and resilient person

Now 21 years old, and with a first-class degree in journalism, Melissa was caring for her mother and stepfather, and providing support for her grandmother and father when she was a child.

'My mum had a lot of health issues and relied on my stepfather to look after her. When I was 10, he fell ill, so the responsibilities fell on me and my eight-year-old sister. We didn't stop to analyse our situation – it was just what we had to do. Washing, cooking, looking after our parents was our way of life.

'Luckily, our school was very supportive – it was actually our teachers who identified us. After that, things became a little easier – we were in the Young Carers in Schools programme and felt that we had adults we could turn to if we were feeling stressed. We also told our closest friends.

'I think the most difficult time was when I was in my teens and I saw my peers going out and splurging on nice clothes and makeup. I couldn't do any of that. It wasn't easy, and I struggled, but I got through it.

'And there were benefits, too. I grew up knowing I could cope with difficulties, that I could take on whatever life threw at me, which made me more resilient. Also, caring for those I loved was rewarding – it boosted my self-esteem, and made me a more independent person.

'That's one of the key messages I want to get across – that there are positives in being a young carer. The other message is that you can get through it, too. Just make sure you talk to people, ask for help and do at least one nice thing for yourself each day, whether it's watching TV, reading a book or going for a walk. Self-care is essential.'

SEEING THE POSITIVE
in every situation

Pretty much everyone's had a time when an event or encounter has left them unhappy and miserable. Perhaps they weren't allowed to go to the cinema with friends, didn't get the result they'd hoped for in an exam or came last in a race at sports day. It can be a rotten feeling.

Negative thoughts can swish around your head, making you feel rubbish or even cause you to say angry and mean things ('I didn't ask to be born!' ring a bell?). But it doesn't have to be that way.

As hard as it may seem, try to think positively, take charge and change the situation to your benefit. For example, if you're grounded, you could use the time to practise an activity you enjoy or want to get better at, like baking cupcakes (see page 34) or drawing a picture.

When it comes to sports day, instead of focusing on who won, who came second and who came last, try to make the most of the opportunity it provides to spend time with friends, being outdoors and getting some fresh air and physical activity. Remember that everyone has different abilities. So, running might not be your strong point, for instance, but you'll have loads of other things where you excel. With this in mind, let's look at transforming a few other seemingly bad situations into much better ones:

Situation

Being paired up with a classmate you don't speak to for group work

You might think: 'It's not fair. I want to be with my friend.'
You could say: 'Great! I've got the opportunity to find out more about this person. I might even make a new friend.'

I'm stupid! Why don't I understand like they do?

EVERYONE LEARNS AT A DIFFERENT PACE. I'M MUCH SMARTER AT MATHS – MAYBE WE COULD SWAP TIPS.

People aren't choosing me because they don't like me.

SO SPORT ISN'T MY STRONG POINT, BUT I'M GREAT AT LOTS OF OTHER THINGS.

Situation

Not getting the lead role in the school play

You might think: 'I knew I wasn't good enough to play the main man. I'm so rubbish.'
You could say: 'Actually, my character's really complicated and so mean. He'll be great fun to play. '

Situation

Not being invited to a student party

You might think: 'They haven't asked me because they don't want to be my friend.'
You could say: 'Some people want to be my friend, others don't. That's OK. There'll be other parties that I'm invited to and they'll be better because my close friends will be there.'

Why can't my parents get me expensive gifts? It's not fair.

MY PARENTS' LOVE FOR ME ISN'T MEASURED BY THE PRESENTS THEY BUY ME.

41

HARNESS THE POWER

How tuning in to your inner voice can help with decision making

Have you ever met someone and felt instantly that they were nice and you wanted to be their friend? Has a new teacher ever walked into the classroom and you knew they were going to be strict before they said a word? Have you solved a maths problem without knowing how you came to your answer? These are all examples of intuition at work.

What exactly is intuition? Intuition comes from the Latin word intueri, which means to look inside or consider. It's when you understand something instinctively without conscious thinking. You might have heard it referred to as a gut feeling or a feeling in the bones.

Intuition is like your own inner compass that can help you to set plans and reach your goals. When you make a decision almost instantly, or an idea or course of action pops suddenly into your head, that's your intuition talking.

Sometimes that inner voice may not be so strong. At school, teaching tends to focus more on utilising skills for analysing and thinking through things consciously. The idea of just knowing something, without being able to explain how you know it, might be considered irrational or unscientific. The lack of focus on developing intuitive skills can make your unconscious voice of inner knowing quieter.

But even some of the most analytical of thinkers have acknowledged the power intuition played in their incredible discoveries. Albert Einstein, considered by many to be the greatest scientist of his age, said: 'The intuitive mind is a sacred gift and the rational mind is a faithful servant.' He thought 'the great scientists are artists as well' and recognised science was a creative act that sometimes involved bypassing the conscious mind and going with gut feelings.

Learning to cultivate your intuition has many benefits. Jean-Luc Boissonneault is an entrepreneur, writer and speaker, who describes intuition as being the highest form of intelligence. 'Intellect is about the knowledge we retain from others,' he says, whereas 'intuition is about work from the heart. Doing something for the right intent. Doing something that matters. Intuition is about creativity.'

When you access intuition, you access a part of yourself that is individual, creative and wiser than your conscious self. It's a tool that can help in all aspects of your life.

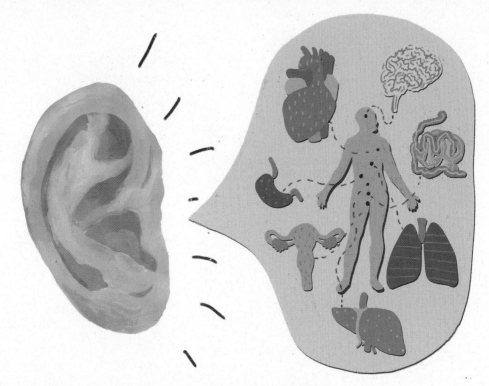

'The intuitive mind is a sacred gift'

ALBERT EINSTEIN

HOW TO TAP INTO YOUR INTUITION

1 Listen to yourself

Listen carefully to your thoughts. Notice when ideas, desires or solutions pop into your head. Get to know your voice of intuition and what it sounds like. Don't dismiss these hunches. For example, if you're up late at night studying and a voice inside your head says 'go to bed, you're overtired now and nothing you're achieving is going to be very productive', then pay attention. This voice most likely knows what you need more than your conscious mind does.

2 Tune into your body

Candace Pert was an American scientist and author of books including *Molecules of Emotion* and *Everything You Need to Know to Feel Go(o)d*. She suggested that the body was in effect the unconscious mind. All emotions are physical, embodied phenomenon. So, when you get a sense of dread in the pit of your stomach or a sudden fluttering in your heart this is important information, a way that your intuition is communicating with you. Don't ignore what your body is trying to tell you.

3 Ask yourself

What is your body trying to tell you? Pose a question to yourself and then listen to whatever pops into your head. Often this first thought is a flash of intuition before rational and reasoning thought takes over.

4 Meditate on a question

If you have a difficult decision to make, it sometimes helps to throw out that list of pros and cons. One study, conducted six months after drivers purchased a new car, revealed that those who had made quick choices were significantly happier with their vehicles than those who'd taken a long time coming to their decision.

Intuition

If you've been deliberating on a question for a while, your mind may have filled up with mental chatter that can make it hard to hear your intuition speak. One way to listen out for your inner voice is to write your question on a piece of paper and then meditate on it. Instead of consciously thinking, open up your mind and ask for the answer to come to you. Then listen out until you can hear it loud and clear.

5 Journalling

Journalling is another way to get through all the mental confusion that can make it hard to hear your intuition. Write down all the thoughts that come into your head as you deliberate on an issue or problem. It can be helpful to vent any fears or worries about taking a particular course of action. Perhaps you're holding back from letting your intuition speak because you're scared of stepping into the unknown.

As you write, pay attention to any sentences that seem to transcend indecision, confusion or fear. These sentences of wisdom are your intuition, and they could hold the key to help you make your decision.

WORDS: KATE ORSON. ILLUSTRATIONS: ANIESZKA BANKS

#FEED YOUR LIFE

Social media can leave you feeling left out or left behind. It can easily generate envy, but what if it could also inspire you to feel better about who you are and what you already have? Here's how you can use your feed to be less like them and more like you…

Facebook and Instagram are like trailers for a film, showing the highlights of people's lives. The photos you see aren't always a true or balanced representation of the bigger picture. It's hard to know what's really going on behind the scenes, and easy to assume the people you follow live super-exciting lives, especially if they're always looking their best and doing things you've never done before.

If you think you're the outsider looking in, know that wanting to be popular, or to belong, is a natural human instinct. That's why it feels so important to be seen, recognised and liked. Since social media provides an easy platform to shout about the events in your life, it can seem like it's the only way to achieve that sense of belonging.

If you're trying too hard to keep up, however, you might focus too much on becoming the person you think you should be, rather than being yourself and doing things that make you happy, which is more likely to help you find really special friends and feel like you truly belong.

WORKING WITH ENVY

If you think of your social media feed as a mirror, it can help you to look past the people who make you envious in order to see the things that could make you happy instead. If you find yourself feeling a sense of envy over someone's friendships, looks or achievements, for example, you could think of these things as reflections of what's possible in your life. In fact, they may already be present, it's just that you haven't known how to find them – until now. *So, take a moment, grab something to write with and try to answer the following questions…*

Is there one particular person who makes you especially envious?

What is it about them that makes you feel this way?

What do they have that you want?

What are they doing that you wish you could do?

Perhaps they're really popular, great at a particular sport or always do well academically. Make a note of your answers and, if you can, narrow them down to a handful of specific attributes or activities.

If the person always seem to look fit and well, for example, it might not be their looks that bother you, but their healthy lifestyle. If they're popular, you may not crave as many friends as they have, but simply to spend more time with people who support and understand you. If someone seems to have something that you don't, it doesn't mean you can't have it too. So once you've got to the root of your envy, you can use this as motivation to make some changes and take steps towards achieving for yourself the things you envy in others.

Too much going on in your feed to single out one person's posts? Turn the page to find out how to be more 'You'.

BE MORE 'YOU'

If your social media feed feels like a constant information overload, it can be difficult to choose just one person who makes you feel envious. If this is the case, there are other ways to cut through the noise and focus on what motivates you. *Here are a few ways you might try to do this…*

1   Look at your feed and pick someone at random. Scroll through their pictures, focusing on the detail that prompts negative emotions. Now, put yourself in their shoes for a moment. How do you imagine you'd feel? Can you turn 'wanting' into 'having'? Can you access more positive emotions?

2   Write down these emotions (you could use the panels here) alongside a list of the things you imagine would make you feel how you want to feel. These could be anything from *'popularity'* to *'better grades'*, *'recognition'* or *'excitement'*. Could you use these words to describe your own life? What's already going well? What could you do to make things better? Maybe you could join a club, spend more time on a hobby or with friends who make you laugh, or ask for more support with your studies.

3   You can even cut your list down to just a handful of words or phrases that feel most important to you. Up to five is a good number. If you keep this list handy, it will remind you why you're envious of certain people, and what you can do about it. Let them be a reflection of all the good things already going on in your life, as well as the great things to come.

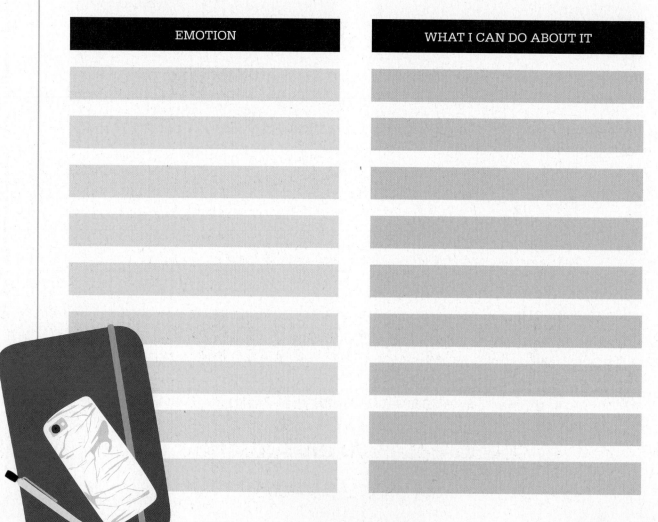

EMOTION	WHAT I CAN DO ABOUT IT

INSTA-ANXIETY

Some posts can have a negative impact without the original poster even knowing it. Are you using social media positively?

Social media is a fantastic way to stay in touch with others and share information. One of the most popular ways to do this is via Instagram, which launched in 2010 as a photo-sharing platform. Now, though, you can use it for more than building a gigantic picture album as you can share videos, Instagram stories, create polls, exchange messages with other users and invite public questions.

Mostly, these are fun, but they can be used to cause upset by online bullies or those thinking they're having 'a bit of banter'. Sometimes, the people doing this have no idea of the turmoil that results, which is why it's important to think about what you post to ensure social media is a positive experience for all – rather than a cause of anxiety.

Don't judge

An image may pop up in an Instagram story with the message 'Like for a rating', and this is one example of how social media can be negative. The poster is basically saying: 'Like this picture and I will judge you on a scale of one to 10'. Usually the rating is based on looks or personality or friendship, but it could be on anything – the poster can decide. Sometimes, the user will send the rating via a direct message (DM), but too often they will post a list of the likes on their page with their judgments or ratings next to them, showing everyone how they 'rate' other people. While this is fine if you get a good rating, it can be mortifying if the user judges you lower than everyone else.

If you're the one posting the 'Like for a rating', you might think it's fun – but consider how each comment or rating could affect the person, especially if it's someone you don't know well. Take into account the fact many people are unconfident about their looks. You may be a brutally honest person, but if you're not going to say anything positive, it's often better not to say anything.

If you're the one who receives a low rating, it will sting but try not to take it personally. This is just one person's judgment and perspective. Who are they to be the ultimate decision maker on who's attractive or what kind of person you are? It will hurt if they've done it publicly, but instead consider that the most important judge of you is you. And after that it's your real friends and family. In future, try not to get sucked into these polls. They rarely end well.

Sharing embarrassing videos

Another negative social media craze is filming others in embarrassing situations and posting the clips online. Often these are quickly liked and shared, causing humiliation for the subject, who may not have been aware they were being filmed. Sometimes, the film may have been set up – for example, tripping up a classmate or quietly pulling their chair away to get a reaction. Those behind the set-up and recording often claim it's just fun or banter, but it could also be considered bullying.

The embarrassment could have a profound impact on the person affected, denting their confidence and causing them a huge amount of stress and anxiety both now and in the future. If you see a video online and like or share it, you're contributing to the situation and it's almost as if you're supporting it. Instead, report the situation to a teacher or family member with the aim of getting the video removed and helping the student involved. Imagine how you'd feel if you were the one being filmed – what would you want to happen? You might think you'd find it funny, but you never know until it happens.

Direct attacks

When someone's angry with another person or just dislikes them, they can easily use social media to be hurtful. Whether it's tagging a student's name onto an insulting photo or writing cruel comments under their post, those with a vendetta can cause instant public humiliation and hurt. A recent feature of Instagram has been the ability to add polls to stories – while these can be used for quick questions, some use them as a means of attacking others, such as posting an image of a person and asking followers if they like them or think they're attractive. For the subject of the polls and posts, it can feel like the whole world is laughing at them – for them, this is cyberbullying.

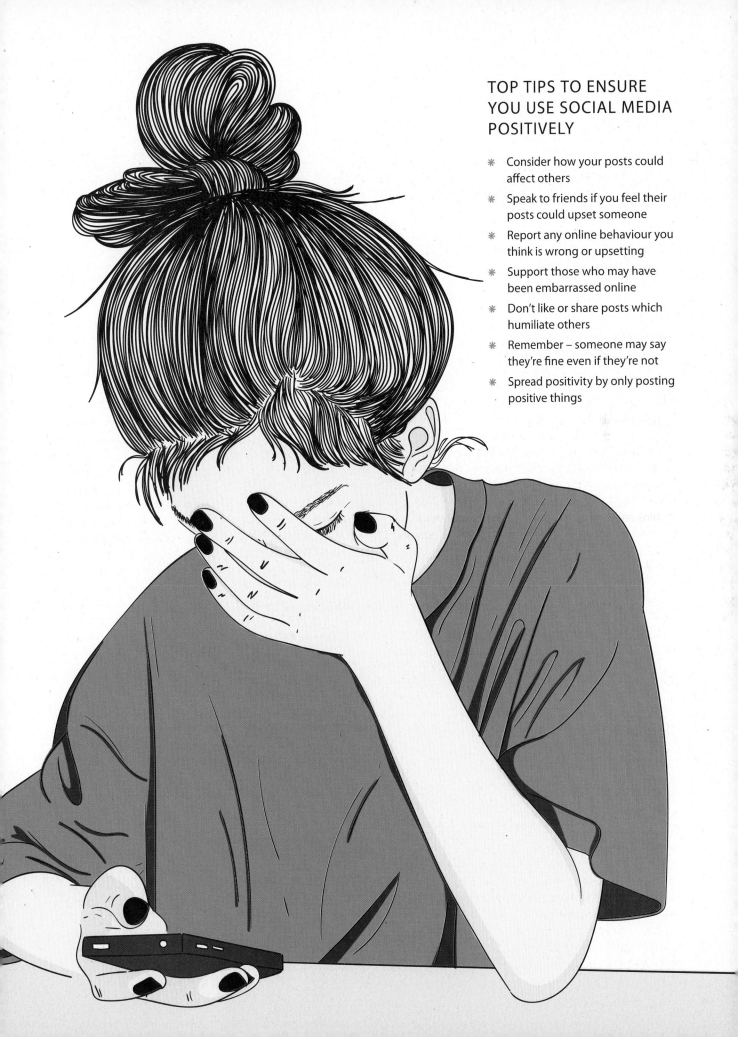

TOP TIPS TO ENSURE YOU USE SOCIAL MEDIA POSITIVELY

* Consider how your posts could affect others
* Speak to friends if you feel their posts could upset someone
* Report any online behaviour you think is wrong or upsetting
* Support those who may have been embarrassed online
* Don't like or share posts which humiliate others
* Remember – someone may say they're fine even if they're not
* Spread positivity by only posting positive things

THINK TWICE

When something bad happens to you, ancient survival instincts can come into play – but mostly it's better to think before you act

Have you heard of the fight-or-flight reflex? It's the way each one of us is wired to react to a perceived threat or harmful encounter. Some people counter-attack and others look for a way to escape. It's a basic element of being human, and probably one that's helped us to survive on this planet for as long as we have – after all, our ancient ancestors would have had to deal with some pretty scary situations.

Life has moved on a lot since prehistoric times – you're no longer likely to come face to face with a sabre-toothed tiger or formidable mammoth while eating dinner, for example. The world is more complex and, even though old instincts remain, sometimes the scary or unsettling situations you find yourself in require different ways of dealing with them.

REFLEX REACTION

There are still some circumstances where those old survival instincts will kick in. Imagine someone puts you in danger. In this case, it's natural to choose, without even really thinking about it, between fighting against or flying from the situation.

If someone pushed you into a wall, for instance, perhaps you'd push back or run away. If you were out riding your bike and a friend started riding dangerously, swerving into you and nearly knocking you off, maybe you'd shout at them to stop.

These responses are driven purely by survival instincts. They help, in a split second, to assess a potentially dangerous situation and ensure self-protection.

But while the fight-or-fight reflex, which stems from a need for self-preservation, makes sense if you're in physical danger, it seems less appropriate in a scenario that involves feelings.

THINK BEFORE YOU ACT

Imagine a different type of situation. Your best friend makes a comment that upsets you, or borrows one of your favourite tops and accidentally spills something on it. Would you react in the same way, by shouting, pushing or running away from the scene ?

Although some of the feelings might be the same – anger, fear and hurt can all cause a knotted feeling in the stomach that leads to lashing out – a calmer reaction might have a better outcome.

Maybe it's better to pause, take a deep breath, process those feelings and explain to your friend that you're upset, and why.

Let's compare what the reaction and the response to this situation might be:

Friend *'Here's your top back, but I splashed something on it and the stain won't come out. I'm sorry, I didn't mean to.'*

You 1 *'What? Why would you do that? That was my favourite top and now it's ruined. I hate you.'*

OR

You 2 *'I'm really upset about that top. It was my favourite and now it's ruined. I know you didn't mean to do it but I'd prefer that you didn't borrow my clothes in future.'*

The first 'you' is reacting from the gut, but it could make a situation that is already unfortunate even worse and lead to more distress. The second 'you' is still making their feelings known, but in a way that's less likely to add fuel to the fire.

Another example: you get a low mark on a maths test at school:

You 1 *'I hate maths. It's the stupidest subject ever and I hate my teacher. She's always picking on me and I bet she failed me on purpose.'*

OR

You 2 *'That's so disappointing, I'm really unhappy. Maybe I'll ask my teacher about it and see what I can do to get a better result next time.'*

The frustration about the low mark completely takes over the first 'you'. Although venting in this way might make you feel better in that particular moment, it's not going to have any benefit in the long term.

Responding to the disappointment is what the second 'you' does. This involves acknowledging how you feel and pinpointing what needs to be done to avoid it happening again.

EMOTIONAL MATURITY

The ability to respond to situations gets easier with experience. If a toddler is told that they can't have ice cream until they finish their dinner, for example, they'll possibly have a tantrum and throw a spoon at the wall. They don't realise it's making their desired outcome even less likely.

A child of six or seven, however, is smarter. They might sulk a bit, but know that after eating carrots (not their favourite), there'll be something altogether tastier on the dinner table.

In other words, teaching yourself to respond, rather than react to disappointment – or hurt feelings – is much more likely to make the end result a positive one.

Don't give yourself a hard time if you do react, rather than respond, to a situation. Everybody has the occasional outburst – just try to follow up with a more considered response after you've given yourself time to process what's happened, how you feel about it and what steps you can take to avoid it being repeated. We can't promise, however, that it'll always result in ice cream.

WORDS: SARAH RODRIGUES. ILLUSTRATIONS: CLAIRE VAN HEUKELOM

HATE IS A BIG WORD…

…and an even stronger emotion. Whether you're on the receiving end of someone's hatred or struggling with such feelings yourself, there are ways of turning it around

Do you often use the 'h' word? 'I *hate* spiders', 'I *hate* peas', 'I *hate* reality television'. These are all harmless statements, often delivered in a casual way, but what happens when such feelings become more than a straightforward dislike and are targeted at another individual or group of people?

What is hate?
Hatred is strong feelings of anger, hostility or resentment towards another person or group. They might even lead to prejudice, discrimination, bullying or violence.

What does it feel like?
An individual who hates might fixate on their enemy, getting pleasure from thoughts of humiliating them or gaining revenge. It can lead to a dark mood, poor judgment and irrational thoughts. Some people might bully, exclude or spread malicious gossip about the target of their hatred.

Why do people hate?
Some negative attitudes might be picked up from friendship groups, family or the media. If those around you have strong negative feelings towards a person or group, you might believe there must be truth in these thoughts, even if it goes against your inner judgment.

These sorts of feelings can often stem from a fear of the unknown. People can dislike others without truly knowing or understanding much about them.

Society can also tend to promote a competitive spirit, so some people may want to show others that they see themselves as better than them. Disliking those who are different reinforces an individual or group's belief that their way of doing things is the right way.

Hate can also emerge from insecurity or jealousy. If you're feeling threatened or experiencing low self-esteem, it can be easy to simply blame others.

WORDS: VICKY H BOURNE. ILLUSTRATIONS: SARA THIELKER

What is a hate crime?

This is a criminal offence in which victims are targeted because they belong to a certain group, for example: because of race, religion, disability, gender identity or sexual orientation. Hate crimes include intimidation, harassment, threats or physical attacks.

If you experience, or witness, a hate incident:

* **Report it**. Tell a trusted adult such as a teacher, school counsellor or nurse or a family member.
* **Put it in perspective**. It doesn't reflect anything you've done but only the other person's prejudice, insecurity or jealousy. Don't let other people's hatred stop you living life to the full.
* **Be active**. If you're a member of an under-represented group and feel confident, ask a teacher if you can give a talk or make a display about your religion or disability to dispel stereotypes.

If you experience strong feelings of hatred:

* **Be kind to yourself**. Everybody has less pleasant thoughts about others from time to time. These can seem more intense when tired or upset. Go for a walk (see page 56), write your thoughts in a journal, have a rest or focus on a hobby. See how you feel afterwards.
Example: 'I was overwhelmed by feelings of hate and anger towards a sibling and began plotting revenge. After football practice and a good night's sleep, I could put it in perspective. I realised I'd been annoyed about an incident at school. A thoughtless comment from my sister had made me target my hate at her.'
* **Realise multiple ways of doing things can all be right.** People convince themselves the way they do things must be right and therefore what other people do must be wrong. In reality, there can be many ways of doing things which are all equally valid.
Example: 'I really hated my netball co-captain who wanted to try out new strategies every match and swap positions all the time. It took me a long time to recognise she had her way of doing things and I had mine. Both were OK, just different.'
* **Ask yourself why you hate.** Sometimes the things people hate about others are things they dislike about themselves. It takes insight and self-awareness to recognise this. Try writing in a journal or talking to a trusted adult. Ask yourself what it is about the other person or group that angers you so much.
Example: 'When I wrote in my journal about my feelings towards a group from a different background, I realised I actually liked all the individuals. Other people around me were prejudiced and I was going along with their ideas. So, I started listening to my own judgment.'
* **Work on your own identity.** Hate can arise from feelings of jealousy, low self-esteem or inadequacy. Move out of this negative spiral by concentrating on building your own strengths, hobbies and connection
Example: 'I hated a group of classmates who seemed to have it all – strong friendships, the latest gadgets, great social lives, good grades and lots of talents. So, I concentrated on my dancing and cultivating my own friendships. I soon found I stopped comparing myself and didn't mind the other group so much.'
* **Get support.** If your feelings are overwhelming or having a negative impact on your life, speak to a school counsellor who is qualified in helping students to cope positively with feelings and emotions.

MATES AND MAD-LIBS

Here at *Teen Breathe* we believe a little appreciation can go a long way. Complete the mad-lib framework here (use the prompts in brackets as a guide) and then read the piece aloud to a good friend to show them how much you care. You could also invent your own framework for that extra-special touch or to see what other friends and family have to say

_____ , my _____ _____ .
(friend's name)   *(adjective)*   *(noun)*

I am so _____ to have you in my life. Let's face it, we go together like
          (emotion)

_____ and _____ ,
(food)   *(drink)*

_____ and _____ ,
(animal)   *(object)*

_____ and _____ .
(person)   *(place)*

Thank you for being you – or in other words – one of the _____ -iest
            (adjective)

people I've ever met. True, you once _____ , but you've also
          (cringy memory)

_____ and _____ .
(sweet memory)   *(sweet memory)*

You may think you're a _____ , but I think you're an absolute
          (adjective, noun)

_____ . As _____ .
(positive noun)   *(author of following quote)*

once said: ' _____ .
          (quote)

WORD GUIDE

Verb: a <u>doing</u> word (e.g. reading, laughing, running)
Adjective: a <u>descriptive</u> word (e.g. meaningful, helpful, funny)
Noun: a <u>name</u>, <u>place</u> or <u>thing</u> (e.g. timetable, London)

COMPILED BY: ABBY COSTEN. IMAGES: SHUTTERSTOCK.COM

STEP BY STEP

'Walking is man's medicine', so said the ancient Greek physician Hippocrates, often referred to as the Father of Western medicine. And it remains the case today. The benefits are numerous – and they're not just physical, especially if you practise mindful walking

What is mindful walking?

Few people pay attention to their surroundings as they dash around every day – be it to school, sports practice, a friend's house or work. Mindful walking can transform these everyday journeys into complete workouts of all five senses. How? By noticing what's going on around you – without judging it – and becoming aware of the sensations that arise as you move. One way to do this is by focusing on one sense at a time while kindly giving that sense all your attention with every step you take.

How can mindful walking improve health?

1 You become physically stronger
Moving more is good for physical health. It stimulates your circulation, the heart and lungs get a workout, the muscles become stronger, and posture improves.

2 You get a brain boost
Taking a break from everyday tasks is like pressing the reset button on the brain. You can return to whatever needs to be done afterwards feeling refreshed and ready to go – even that English project you've been pushing to one side might feel more straightforward.

3 You can manage emotions
Focusing on the present moment allows you to step away from situations that may feel as though they're constantly swirling around in your mind, causing you stress or anxiety. This helps you to distance yourself from any unpleasant emotions the situation may be causing and to shift your perspective.

Joanna Jeczalik, an Oxford-based mindfulness and yoga teacher, loves to encourage students to move more mindfully in their everyday lives. 'Just noticing how your body moves with each new step and connecting with your breathing is therapeutic,' she explains. 'The extra benefit of noticing all the amazing things around you is a lovely way to feel the present moment.'

Mindful walking: one step at a time

Take a while to focus on each of the senses
* **What can you see?** A pretty tree or interesting shadow?
* **What can you hear?** Chirping birds, buses going by or, on a quiet walk, perhaps the sound of your own breath?
* **What can you feel?** A gentle breeze between your fingers or the sensation of pebbles underfoot?
* **What can you taste?** Roll your tongue around your teeth and concentrate. Can you detect the mint of toothpaste or the last vestiges of a lunchtime snack?
* **What can you smell?** Freshly baked bread, new Tarmac?

Take some time to reflect on your experience, how did it make you feel? Start thinking about your next walk. The beauty of mindful walking is that it can be done anywhere. Plan ahead to make sure it's safe and enjoyable.

* Choose a public area that you're familiar with
* Let someone know your route and what time you expect to return
* Take your mobile phone with you – on mute while walking to avoid digital distractions
* Take care around roads and remain aware of traffic
* Don't walk in darkness
* Take a drink with you if it's a particularly warm day

Make it sociable
Mindful walking is a great way to connect with others in a different way. Invite a friend along or even make it a family occasion. Share the role of leader, allocating a minute or two to guide the group through each sense. Each can take it in turns to play back their experiences while the rest of the group listens. Author and *Teen Breathe* writer Kate Orson says: 'Listening can be an act of generosity. Not just for the person being heard, but for the listener too. When you listen you get to stop, and simply be. Doing it well can help to build trust and deepen friendships.'

Give mindful walking a try for yourself to enjoy the here and now, one step at a time.

WORDS: SIMONE SCOTT. ILLUSTRATION: SARAH WILKINS

Happy when it rains

It's easy to understand why some people complain or feel down when it starts to rain. Those brooding, dark clouds overhead have the potential to dampen the mood of even the most cheery of souls. Then, when the rain arrives – producing anything from a fine drizzle or sharp shower to a seemingly endless monsoon-type downpour – it can spoil plans for making the most of being outdoors.

Wet hair, muddy shoes and being soaked to the skin – none of this sounds like much fun. Yet there's something truly beautiful about the rain and if you start to look at it differently, you might begin to appreciate it and, perhaps, even love a rainy day. Now, where are those wellies and an umbrella?

When it rains, there's nothing you can do about it – so you might as well make the most of the weather. You can learn to love everything about a rainy day by shifting your perspective and changing your outlook.

The author John Updike once said that 'rain is grace; rain is the sky descending to the earth; without rain, there would be no life'. How true. Rather than focusing on gloomy thoughts about the damp weather, marvel at its many benefits and beauty.

Watch how rain falls, creating pools and streams on the ground. Enjoy listening to the pitter-patter, splash or torrent of water. Notice how fresh everywhere around you looks after a good downpour. If you find yourself caught out in a shower, enjoy the sensation of raindrops on your skin. Jump in the puddles that have formed. Smell the rain-freshened air. Realise that despite the inconvenience of getting drenched, being outside in the rain can be invigorating and you'll soon dry off when you're back indoors.

You might even learn to love the rain so much that you'll be one of the special group of people known as pluviophiles. Finding joy and peace of mind during rainy days, a pluviophile relishes being outdoors in a shower without an umbrella and they look up at grey skies to welcome those first raindrops.

RAINY DAYS ARE GOOD BECAUSE...

1 If you've no plans to go anywhere, there's suddenly a wonderful opportunity to snuggle up indoors with a hot beverage while reading a book or watching a favourite film. This can be a perfect time for some essential pampering, writing in your journal or catching up on all the tasks you've been putting off for a while.

2 It can be enjoyable and refreshing to be outdoors in the rain. In warmer months, walking while it's raining can bring welcome coolness. During colder times, going outside dressed in wellies and waterproofs can be exhilarating, making you feel more alive.

3 Listening to the sound of rain as it falls can be relaxing, calming and comforting. Take a nap or close your eyes to meditate. This is a perfect time to drift away and dream.

4 Rain is, of course, a crucial part of the cycle of life. It replenishes the earth, helping plants, flowers and trees to grow. A deluge of rain fills the rivers and reservoirs, providing essential water to live and thrive.

5 With a little imagination, those raindrops can be seen as full of mystery and magical qualities. Let them spark your ingenuity and inspire creativity. Some amazing original ideas can arrive during a rain storm.

6 Everything looks fresh, clean and sparkly afterwards. Have you noticed the pleasant, earthy scent that is produced when rain falls on soil or pavements? This is called petrichor and is especially noticeable immediately after a shower following a long period of dry weather.

7 Rain helps you appreciate life and fine-weather days even more. It awakens you, stimulates the senses and enables you to see the Earth as a beautiful planet.

MY RAINY DAY DIARY

The next time it rains, pause for a while and take notice. There are many types of rainfall to enjoy: drizzle, mizzle (fine rain that forms a mist), sharp showers, a spit, a deluge, thundery showers and torrential rain that goes on for hours. Listen to the beat and rhythm of the rain as it falls. Watch the shape and movement of raindrops on windows. See how the water creates puddles, gullies and spray. Go out and feel the rain on your face. Splash your feet in puddles. Do a rain dance. Be grateful for the beauty and life-giving properties of water, and then use this space to explain – in words or pictures – what you noticed and how it made you feel.

TIME TO READ

Curl up on a rainy winter's day with a good book

The long, light evenings of summer may seem like a distant memory, but don't despair. Winter's chilly nights provide the perfect backdrop to some brilliant books and it's the ideal time of year to indulge in something as atmospheric as it is absorbing so, grab a hot drink, settle in a comfy chair, and take your pick from some of these seasonal delights.

First and foremost, let's talk ghost stories. The dark has long been associated with the mysterious and unknown, and if you enjoy letting your imagination run riot among the shadows, you'd do well to invest in a copy of Ransom Riggs' bestseller *Miss Peregrine's Home For Peculiar Children*. The photos in this book add to the quirkiness and creepiness of the overall reading experience (it's probably not a tale for the faint-hearted, mind).

A far more grounded mystery, Sophie McKenzie's multi-award-winning *Girl, Missing* sees adopted teenager Lauren Matthews embark on a journey to find out who she really is. It has to be said that this emotional thriller does tend to divide opinion but those who love it, REALLY love it and, best of all, it's easy to devour in a single sitting – so well worth a read on a dark and rainy day.

If you're after more of a long-term commitment there are lots of great series to choose from too. Let's face it, with the cold weather set to stay until well into the New Year, there's more than enough time to dedicate to something weighty and substantial.

A really good series or saga can give any TV drama box set a run for its money, and Terry Pratchett's comic-fantasy *Discworld* is one of the best-known. Made up of a whopping 41 books, it'll no doubt come as a relief to hear that it's not necessary to read them in order (suggested reading orders can be found all over the internet). *The Colour of Magic* is considered a good place to start, but *Wintersmith* – the story of a witch who unwittingly plays havoc with the seasons – is book number 35, a great introduction, and just right for this time of year.

Much-more manageable in terms of size is Phillip Pullman's *His Dark Materials* trilogy. Controversial,

captivating and beautifully written, this is truly epic literature, with a good dollop of philosophy, theology and physics included to boot. And, if you've already read the three main books, the good news is that there are two shorter novels – *Lyra's Oxford* and *Once Upon a Time in the North* – set in the same universe, plus *The Book of Dust* – the first part of an accompanying trilogy – which has just been published in paperback.

Equally thought-provoking, if somewhat shorter, is *An Eagle in the Snow* by Michael Morpurgo. A piece of historical fiction, it revolves around the tale of a World War One hero, the decisions he made and how they affected many lives. Based on a true story, the moral dilemma at the heart of this book makes it perfect for group reading and talking about with friends.

For something more light-hearted, try Gail Carriger's *Etiquette and Espionage: Finishing School* series. Set in and around Mademoiselle Geraldine's Finishing School for Young Ladies of Quality – an academy with a difference – the four books in this series promise steampunk and assassins, with a good sprinkling of silliness.

For more serious crime-lovers, favourites such as Agatha Christie and Arthur Conan Doyle continue to enthral. Fans of the Sherlock Holmes mysteries should look out for American author Brittany Cavallaro's Charlotte Holmes' books (the first of which is *A Study in Charlotte*).

Here, the teen descendants of Baker Street's finest duo – Sherlock Holmes and John Watson – take up where their forebears left off, using logic and genius to solve classic murder mysteries.

But winter isn't all about things that go bump in the night. It's also a time for magic and make-believe and, if there's one author who teaches us that fairy tales are not just for children, it's Neil Gaiman.

You may already have seen the film adaptations of his engaging and layered fantasy stories *Stardust* and *Coraline,* but the books are still wonderful in their own right. With all the darkness and wonder of the Brothers Grimm, these really are modern masterpieces.

The Sleeper and the Spindle – Neil's collaboration with illustrator Chris Riddell – is a must for those looking for something as beautiful as it is beguiling. A treat for your bookshelves, and well worth adding to your Christmas list.

Finally, for bookworms who'd rather have a range of stories to choose from, *Winter Magic* – an anthology of seasonal tales edited by author Abi Elphinstone, who also has a story of her own in the book – is full of fabulous, short reads from award-winning writers and is sure to be appreciated by all ages for many years to come.

Whichever books you choose to curl up and read with this winter, may they be enchanting, enlightening and, above all else, enjoyable.

TRUE BLISS: A LIE-IN

After a week of early starts, switch off your alarm and make the most of that extra time in bed come Saturday morning

1 As you begin to feel yourself waking, make a conscious decision to keep your eyes closed. Lay on your back and become aware of your breathing. Try to keep it slow and relaxed, paying attention to how your chest rises and falls with each inhalation and exhalation.

2 Is your room hot or cold? Is there a breeze coming through an open window or is the air still? Notice the warmth (or chill) and how it feels on any parts of you that are outside the covers.

3 Listen to the beat of the house. Are any other family members already up and around? Perhaps the whoosh of the shower is a tell-tale sign that an older sibling is getting ready for work or the dog barking excitedly means Mum's just picked up its lead and they're about to head out for a walk.

4 Are any smells wafting up the stairwell and under your bedroom door? Is there a suggestion of coffee brewing or maybe a hint of bacon sizzling under the grill?

5 Think about what you might like to do for the day. It could be you're going to need to get up soon and get ready for footie practice or dance class, or you might have a gloriously unfilled schedule.

6 Open your eyes and let the room come into focus. Is the sun coming through the gaps between your curtains and the window frame?

7 Take a few more conscious breaths. Then, when you're ready, lift the covers and let the weekend begin.